Inventing Telephone

By Sue Graves

Long ago there were no telephones. Instead people used a telegraph to communicate. It sent electricity through wires.

Telegraph operators used this part of the telegraph to send messages.

Electricity from the telegraph made clicks. The clicks stood for letters. Telegraph operators knew how to turn the clicks into messages.

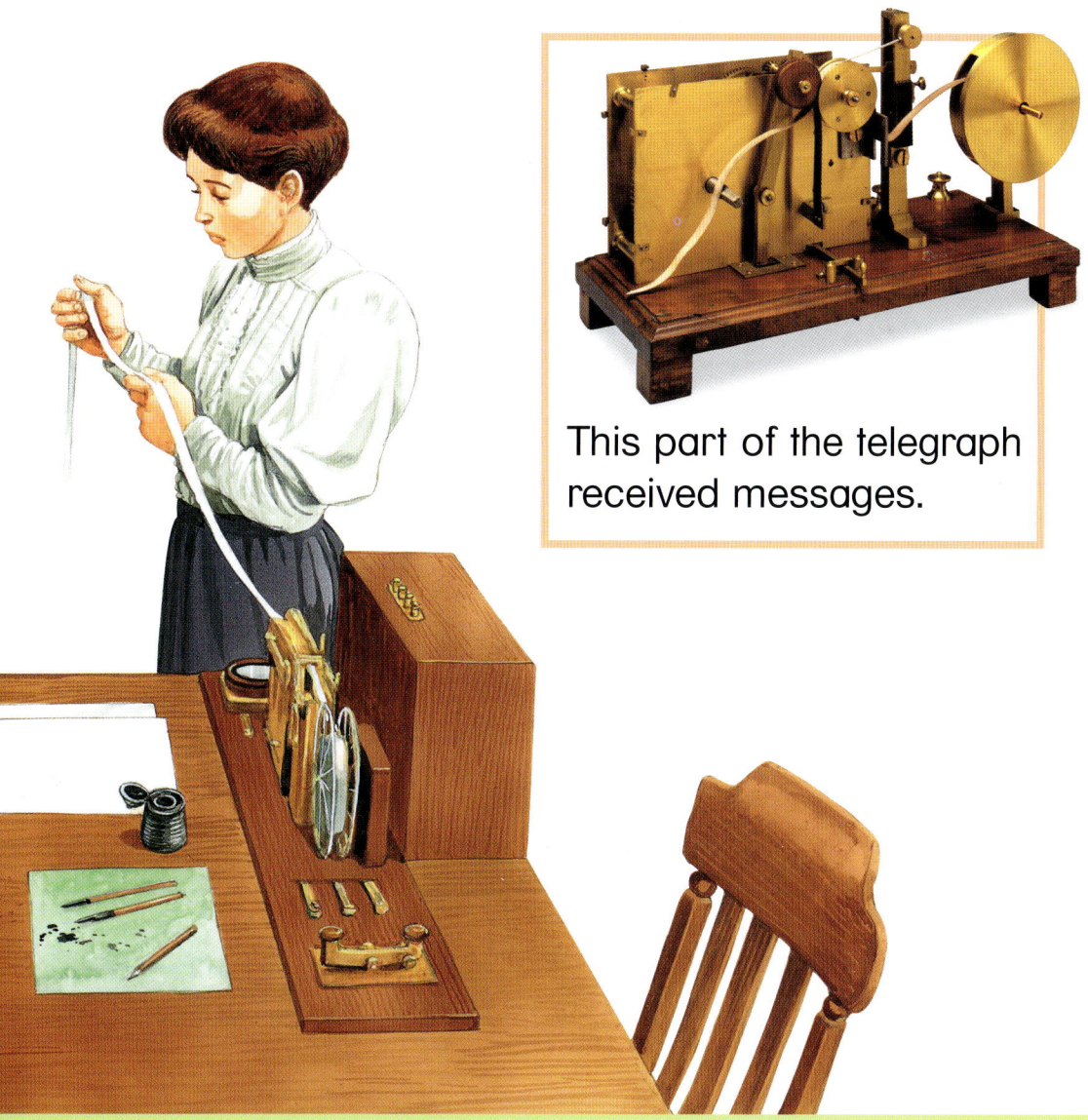

This part of the telegraph received messages.

Alexander Graham Bell was interested in the telegraph. He thought he could make it better.

Bell knew that electricity from the telegraph made clicks. He thought that electricity could make voice sounds, too.

Thomas Watson was Bell's helper.
One day he was fixing Bell's telegraph, when it made a noise.

Bell was in a different room. He heard the noise through the wires. Now Bell was sure electricity could send voices through wires, too.

Bell and Watson's first telephone

Bell and Watson got to work. They started to make a machine that used electricity to send voices. It was the first telephone.

Bell's first telephone did not work well.
Watson spoke into the telephone.
But Bell could not hear him.

Bell and Watson kept trying. They drew pictures. They used the drawings to make a better telephone.

On 10th March 1876 Bell was working on the new telephone. He wanted to tell Watson something. "Mr Watson, come here. I want you!" he called.

Watson heard him through the telephone in the next room. The new telephone worked.

The first successful telephone

Bell and Watson travelled around the country with their new invention. They showed people how to use it.

Over the years telephones have become much better. Many telephones don't need wires any more. Today telephones can be used in many places.

1876　　　1920s　　　1930s

Index

Bell, Alexander Graham 4, 5, 6, 7, 8, 9, 10, 11, 13

clicks 3, 5

electricity 2, 3, 5, 7, 8

telegraph 2, 3, 4, 5, 6

telegraph operators 2, 3

telephone 2, 8, 9, 10, 11, 12, 14–15

telephones over the years 14–15

Watson, Thomas 6, 8, 9, 10, 11, 12, 13

wires 2, 7, 14